ONLY FLYING

BROOK BHAGAT

For information contact:
Unsolicited Press
Portland, Oregon
www.unsolicitedpress.com
orders@unsolicitedpress.com
619-354-8005

Cover Design: Kathryn Gerhardt
Editor: Alexandra Lindenmuth

ISBN: 978-1-950730-83-4

TABLE OF CONTENTS

THE MAMMOTH   5

YOU WERE BORN IN BUTTERFLY   7

ECLIPSE   11

I GET FOUND, 1974   12

THE SAME WOMAN (SCARLIGHT)   14

JUMP (MAGIC PANTS)   16

THE SKY OF THE SKY   18

WAVESTAR BANG   20

THE RIVER'S HARP   21

THE LEFT EYE IS ENOUGH   27

DOWNWELLING   28

I FOUND A PAIR OF HANDS DIGGING IN THE
     GARDEN   30

THE STAR AND THE CROP   33

THERE IS A MOTHER WAITING FOR YOU, A
     KANGAROO   34

POCKET HOLLOW   36

SHE COMES IN ON A PEAHEN   37

THE WAY THE WORLD ENDS   40

SEVEN NOTES   41

THE GOBLIN KING SLIPS AN EMPTY STRING   45

THE WATERFALL   46

THE WEST WING   48

THE LADY SCARECROW   49

SOFT FRACTURE   50

ONCE UPON A TIME I DIED   51

MARS KISSES CLING HARD   54

THE FISHERMAN'S GAZE   55

THE WIDOW'S CAT   57

THE MASTER   58

THE EDGE OF THE WOODS   59

GRANDMA'S EGG   61

GOOD DREAM BAD DREAM   65

CHAPTER TWENTY-SIX: THE MAP   66

NIGHTSHIRT   70

CIRCLE, HEART, CROCODILE, RIVER   71

I'M BUILDING A HOUSE ON THE RAILROAD

    TRACKS   74

PUBLIC POEMS BUILT ON PUBLIC PROPERTY   75

THE GOLDEN THREAD   76

WOKE UP THIS MORNING   79

WE ARE APRICOT TREES   86

ONLY FLYING   89

for Grandma Muriel
for planting the seed of writing in me
and watering it with love my whole life

THE MAMMOTH

You can't do it. You are too small, too fat, too thin, too broken. You are not dressed, and your father is not with you. How can you ride the mammoth?

You will twist the auburn fur in your shaking fists. Your heart will quicken and the musk will repel and excite you, make your body know how far you are from home. You will hear the grunts and huffs and see how it shifts its weight; you will imagine losing everything, but you will not turn back this time. You will plant your naked feet in the right places—thigh, third rib, left shoulder. You will remember the magic words and whisper in its ear: "Carry me gently, Beast of Earth; carry me gently, Beast of Fire. Carry me gently and I will owe you; carry me gently and I will love you."

You will feel the sweat of the beast penetrate your pores. You will relax the barrier of your skin, open your chest to the monster, expose all your secrets and weaknesses. You will feel the marrow of the mammal mixing with your own and stop insisting on difference. You will let the fences in your mind blaze and admit they were made of paper, always on the verge of burning.

Perhaps you will fail and be killed. Perhaps you will be thrown, trampled, crushed, impaled with tusks through your very center. Perhaps you will soil yourself before you die, and everyone will see.

Perhaps your father will die before you, or your mother, or your beloved, or your child. Perhaps they will leave you some other way. Perhaps it will be your fault.

Yet, remember, the animal may feel your defenseless essence and find you worthy. It may trust your promise, let you ride. The fear may begin to fade, and you may find your balance. You may feel the rhythm of its breath rising and falling with your own, and you may savor the warmth of its body on your underside. You may enjoy the fragrance of flowering trees as you pass and the view from the height of its back. It may become your familiar, and you may ride with closed eyes and send it wordless messages that only it could understand, and it may share its infinity with you. You may lay belly-down on its neck, and it may know you better than your father, or your mother, or your beloved, or your child.

It may know when you are ready before you do, and it may begin to run.

YOU WERE BORN IN BUTTERFLY

Maybe you remember that you are a seeker.
Maybe you carved it on your wrist
or on a sign around your neck. Maybe
you made a business card of it
wrote it on a rabbit's foot
or whispered it into your secret pocket.

Maybe you have forgotten, and you laugh
at these types with their bare feet
and empty guitars.
It doesn't really matter.
You were. You are.
Just listen, and try to remember:
You were born in Butterfly.

Relax into it; it will be easier near
the water. Sit down in the shower, sit down
by the gutter. Watch how the lines pull
and become the other, feel
how they melt and disappear.

You were born in Butterfly, between the river
to the west and the river to the east,

heir to the throne and fortune. Yet
the day came when you looked straight
through those golden mirrors
and the silver chalice dropped from your hand.

You closed the flowering harem doors,
sent all those budding gods and goddesses
back to their villages.
You shaved your glorious hair
and left the palace naked,
refusing the money, the satchel
and your mother's tears. You refused the blanket
and even the begging bowl:
You had to know if your hands would do.

You walked beyond walking,
eyes down, eyes up.
You waded through cities and towns.
You became a stranger to the world,
a gray thing in the marketplace,
a hollow stem cupping alms without asking.

You crumbled, slivered, shattered, mad.
And then you came back,
leaving the pieces there by the roadside.

When you learned to fold your thoughts
into an iron ball
and drop it to the bottom of the ocean
the clouds opened for the moon.
Your mind had nothing left to say
as you came to the edge of the river,
crossed and walked to the mountain.

You drank from springs hidden in thickets,
ate fruit from unlikely trees.
As you climbed higher,
the air became thin
but you were able to breathe.

Without map or master, you found
the cave of legend at dawn,
stood at the mouth and smiled
to see fear could still touch you.
You took the step, and went in alone.

You ran your fingers along the wall,
colder and wetter the deeper
you went. Black became blacker
and just before you disappeared,
you thought of turning back.

Then you fell, and I think
you know the rest.
It was right to forget, but now
it's right to remember:
You were born in Butterfly.

ECLIPSE

Night after night I climb out
the same window, light
a cigarette in the snow
and look for home.

I GET FOUND, 1974

My beloved was born with a pebble in his hand,
a red stone burning.
He dropped it in the moment
between the womb and the catching,
the landing in hands,
twisted down for just a blink
and let it go.

Still gleaming from the quilt
of beyond, woven thick with invisible threads,
it melted a hole in that sea-green marble
Rajasthani hospital floor like butter it

burned through the street,
the sandstone
limestone
water and soil,
the heavy metal fishbowl
at the center of the earth.
Then granite, granite,
flint and feldspar
aquifer and dirt again.

It sizzled straight up through red-white cotton,
their Rocky Mountain picnic blanket
and sailed five feet in the air before gravity
caught it, sent it
tumbling back down
through my mother's hippie hair.

It landed like jasmine in her lap

and I was born with a pebble
in my hand.

THE SAME WOMAN (SCARLIGHT)

I wasn't following her I was

just going the same way down

the grocery store pasta aisle, little green
dress bounce dance grass Converse

doublestep gone down despite
wounds bare

legs gingham cotton
dancing skipping young young

Is she? Down checkerboard linoleum
down Thursday, desire

nestled in boxes, pictures
of little red tomatoes.

Then her scars pulled tight
across the back of her knees,

recent bud rose like she should've still been

wearing bandages. The caterpillar

left wound was vertical and she cried
when the stitches broke free and flew away

but she kept on dancing
let them tear

and instead of blood

        light came out.

JUMP (MAGIC PANTS)

They sway in the night, clear in the cold sodium vapor, not leather but thick and hard like someone's old skin, beast housing. Gold stitching laces the fly and the lines between stripes that you follow with your eyes, guilty, running in swirls around the hips, down the ass and out the Hendrix flares at the bottom: hot pink, cherry, blacklight blue. One belt loop is broken.

They aren't meant for you. From the moment you see them, hanging stiff from the fire escape, you know they are for a different kind of person altogether. Keep walking, you tell yourself. They don't look like your size, and you feel like a fraud, a tight-throated imposter in someone else's dream as you hop the chain-link, step on the wooden crate and pull yourself up onto the rusting Dumpster. You're not high enough, and you'll have to jump to grab them. It's going to be loud and it's going to echo down the alley, waking up the neighborhood. Your heart is banging in your ears and you can't think and you don't know how you got here but you know you'll have to run if you do it, and it's not like you at all.

You've come this far. You start to see yourself in them, and you always wanted to be a different person, someone who wears fringe and Hendrix flares and laughs at danger. You breathe in tremors and squint at the dark dirty windows, stretching like holes up to the furry sky. You smell your hands: Nasty.

You do it. You squat spring up jump and snatch them from the railing and when you land on the metal you revel in the live vibration for one slow motion second before the fear hits and you fall slide down to the gristle pavement and scramble up again, the scaly fabric clutched in your fist like a backwards salvation. Lights snap open square jaws in a flick flick flick yellow shades zinging up flash flash flash *Motherfucker took my pants!*

You run for it, down the alley, right at the street, not looking back. Slap slapping feet hammer at your back *Come back!*

Down down around and up the block in and out turn and your knee is screaming, door and stairs and home shaking for the key and you're in, bolt it, chain it, lock the door. Did you lose him? You've seen the movies and you should be thinking about a way out if the fist comes pounding through the but instead your back slides down the wall and you finger them, turn them, smell them: some strange sweetness. You should be thinking about a way out, but you strip.

It's not like you. You hate yourself and you love yourself as you pull them on, buttonhole and zip the zip. You stand up and run your hands tight on the thighs. They fit.

THE SKY OF THE SKY

I thought the meadow's thread would hold,
sewn to my back pocket, invisible
to the outside world. It trailed along
in the ether of a different atmosphere
pulling my hiding place, a weightless
layer of earth and wildflowers. I would
climb it when I was light,
early morning alone, toes
gripping buttons, beads, and knots
and part the bracken at the top.

Nestled forever in late spring,
dragonflies crossed cicadas in my private
sky of the sky, sketching the edges
of the circle, ringed with aspens. A blue gypsy
horse would be napping there, a mare
who let me lean on her as I read,
let me dream with her of wheatgrass pastures
and honeycrisp apples hanging low.

Held with only a clove hitch
to a thistle, the thread gathered soot
as I thought through the city, forgot

everything real. I found it loose, dead
on the ground but

when thunderstorms come I can still
make out the roots in the sky
on the underlings of clouds like
magnets dragging iron filings.
They show the way and one day

I will climb the lightning

and never come back.

WAVESTAR BANG

He lost her, but not as he thought: not to the cancer, or a car accident, or to some art student.

She was dancing alone, a whirling wavestar in the dark, only the nightlight of the stove etching her naked toes, her knees, her swirling hips. She spun, hair whipping, neck caning, hands open as autumn leaves whose time had come.

She became transparent, spinning faster and faster. She evaporated from the feet up, a tornado of silver steam.

He fell right through her.

THE RIVER'S HARP

Before the hospital, Kuan was sleeping in the park. Or maybe the dinosaur man had let her sleep on the floor of his room that night.

She had to meet someone to play harmonica at sunset at a bar called Heroes, on the west side of the Coyote River. It was her destiny, but she couldn't get a ride, and the sun was touching the hills.

The bridge was a thundering highway with a six-inch curb between the cars and the rail. It was not a sidewalk. The sun hit her eyes but her mind and blood thrilled, beamed as she stepped on, cars shrieking, blurring past: silver black blue black silver red red. She thought of the story, of how it would be written: *she walked on foot, fearlessly, over the bridge.*

She stepped off on the other side ten minutes later and followed a footpath, curling down the bank. She sat on a bed-sized rock, looked across the river, and there it was: HEROES, in neon red and blue. On the east side of the river.

She laughed and laughed, thinking how beloved she was. God loved her this much. It was a hilarious joke, and God had nothing better to do than to play with her! She laughed until her stomach hurt, loving being chosen.

"I'm not going back across that bridge!" she yelled, shaking her finger and grinning up at the sky, gathering clouds for evening.

Sunbeams bounced in the river. She could hear the water, smell its fishy smell. The idea came to her in a tingle: *I'll swim across the goddamn river* (she liked to swear just to tease Him). *She swam across the Coyote River.*

Sidestepping down the steep dirt and grass to the water, she thought of what they would call her: *Hail Kuan, full of face* (her face was round and flat, a yin-face, her mother said). *It will not just be a prayer this time around. It will be the first song I play at all my concerts.*

She scrambled down and stopped near a dying bush. She thought of the story again. *My brother had a crown of thorns; Kuan had thistles in her hair.* She pulled a dry, hay-colored thistle off the plant, a little ball of spikes. She snarled it into her long black hair, just behind her ear, and then another and a third, rolling them into tangles. She had to do it as an act of faith, of acceptance of her destiny, all sides.

Black tank top and cutoffs, her harmonica in her front pocket. She took off her shoes and left them there, thinking, *she took off her shoes and left them there.*

She waited for a barge to go by and stepped in, the water cool and easy. She loved to swim, and the current was not enough to sweep her anywhere. She would reach the other side half a block downstream, maybe.

When she was in the middle, a little speedboat came by, a family with two boys. "Are you ok?" the man called.

"I'm fine. I'm just swimming."

"Do you want to get out?" he asked, steering the boat closer.

I should let them "rescue" me, Kuan thought. *He is a kind man, and it will be an honor for their family. They will become part of the story.* "Yes," she said.

They took her to the east bank, where she waved goodbye from the shore. They all four waved back, and she climbed up the embankment to Heroes, a single-story bar.

She paused at the top. Music sang from inside: twelve-bar blues, a vibration in her fingertips and electric skin. Then the wind picked up, chilling every hair on her wet body. "I'm going, I'm going!" she said, cocking her head up at the sky and smiling. She fingered the harp in her pocket, closed her eyes and filled her lungs: *Kuan closed her eyes and filled her lungs.*

At the dinosaur man's mirror, in the front room, Kuan had seen the history of every molecule in her body: The slave. The wanderer. The hermit. The soldier—tears and shaking the night she remembered Auschwitz. She screamed and threw her combat boots out the window, even though it was so long ago. The large animal, the small animal. The rock. *I was the dirt in the Garden*, she thought, swaying to the beat. *Hail Kuan, full of face. Hallowed be Thy name.* The burden of knowledge was great, but her joy was greater.

Kuan went in to Heroes living each moment as it was written. She danced like a forest fire, spinning mad and thoughtless, crouching, jumping free and wild, blowing every last drop of herself through the harp. "Stay in D!" she yelled at the band. "The only key I've got is D!"

The guys laughed and drank and did as they were told. The music and crowd spilled out the front doors into the street, following Kuan, who needed more space to dance. The sun moved farther and farther away from her side of the earth, and finally she had to stop. She had to drink water. When she caught her breath, she realized she was shivering with sweat, hair and clothes still wet from the river.

"Who will give me the shirt off his back?" Kuan yelled at the crowd.

"I will," grinned a broad-shouldered man on a motorcycle. "Come here." He crossed his arms and took off his T-shirt, revealing muscles and nipples that stiffened in the night air.

Kuan's heart began to writhe. *It's the Devil,* she thought. *The Devil gave her the shirt off his back.*

She walked over to the motorcycle, took the shirt, and put it on. "Get on," he said. The crowd and the musicians called to her, telling her not to go, but she knew she had no choice. *It was her destiny.*

The man drove to an empty park on the other side of town. They walked together in silence to a picnic table under a gazebo, out of sight of the road. Mosquitoes orbited a solitary lamppost, buzzing yellow-orange. Kuan sat on the table and tried to take the thistles out of her hair, which had begun to hurt her scalp. "Can you help me?" she asked.

The man's hands touched her hair and her head. Kuan saw the strands from the corner of her eye and felt the pulling. She asked if it was working. The man stepped back and laughed, watching her face as her hands went up. "You made it worse!" she said.

The man laughed again and grabbed her, squeezing her arms. He forced her down onto the table on her back and tried to pull down her cutoffs. Kuan kicked him in the chest with both feet. He fell back onto the grass and glared up at her.

Kuan held out her arms. "I am your mother," she said, looking deep in his eyes. "I forgive you." They were not just words. They were not a strategy to escape. She summoned all her divine love and saw the child in him.

The man growled and rushed at her, this time tearing the shirt down the side. Again she fought off his body and then loved his soul. "I am your mother," she said again, opening her arms. "I forgive you."

"Stop saying that!" spat the man. "You're not my mother, you crazy bitch!"

"But I am your mother," Kuan said, knowing the truth of her words, knowing that she was the mother of the world. "It's all right. I forgive you."

Again and again he charged at her. She resisted each attack with her arms and legs, but without anger, without panic or fear. Again and again she repeated her prayer with love, rose to her feet, and offered her embrace, looking into his glacier eyes. At last, she saw something crack in them.

"Fucking crazy bitch," he said, wiping blood from his lip. "You're not fucking worth it."

"I'm proud of you," she said.

He snorted and left.

Kuan heard the motorcycle drive away. She touched her bruises, the thistles, and the tender bump on the back of her head, and beamed up at the night sky, loving her story.

THE LEFT EYE IS ENOUGH

Because you can see. It was other people who had the problem. Pros and cons blink in unison; flies cannot understand singular vision. Dark glasses and patches insult the blind and pirates. Suits and snoots on the train and even the grubs on the street shot feary scowls and snickers, sideways sneers and whispers. The nothingness bothered them, the absence of the right, smooth as burned-off fingerprints. They were not convinced by your best prosthetic and tossed you pity, a reward for your emulation of their emulation of normalcy. Your final answer is the biggest lie by the bluntest knife: a wound.

DOWNWELLING

We are adrift, adrift
throw me clear, bone
China teacup sharps
pieces pieces out the window

Swells and whitecaps
I flutter down the water
triggerfish, triggerfish
barriers and reefs

I settle on the bottom
of the ocean,
wedged in sand, apart

we can see the other
but not touch, relics
like the lifeboat
the pirate ship and the

Good Ship Jesus
dragging cold currents,
winding the warped
wooden phonograph

still hung with Strange Fruit
after all these years,
Our Lady of the Flowers
singing pieces
through the water

so low, so low,
both with me

and alone.

I FOUND A PAIR OF HANDS
DIGGING IN THE GARDEN

I was looking for eyes but I found a pair of hands
digging in the garden. They fit quite better than mine
and I have been wearing them ever since.

I found a teacup digging in the garden. When I tried
to empty it, I found a tiny woman swimming through the soil,
living like a worm in the little round room.

I thumbed across the surface and her head and neck emerged.
She was smooth and translucent, eyeless, earless,
diving out of the dirt and back in again like a dolphin.
I picked her up by the scruff and held her inches from my face
but she remained unaware, squirming, singing, moaning. I
wanted to take her home,
keep her in the windowsill and make her happier,
plant some coriander for her like trees or even
make her a new place, a shoebox with a carpet of soil
and a little raisin box for a flat-screen TV.
I won't make her a bed, I thought,
she will always prefer to sleep in the dirt
and then I let her go.

I found the alley cat digging in the garden, biting at the beets
and scratching at the soil. She has no tail. She is sharper
and faster than the housecats. I have heard her fight
in the alley. I have seen her sit still and silent in the lightning
tree like an old crow. She has never belonged to anybody
but herself.

She has been in our yard before. I backed away,
opened the door slowly, fetched a dish of cream for her,
like I have done before. She took one look
at me and the cream and
bolted over the fence, like she has done before.

I found a key digging in the garden, rusted with a red ribbon
decomposing around its neck. I fancied that it did not fall
out of a pocket by accident. I fancied it was the key
of a Lover who had been Lost. I rubbed it with my thumb
and the metal was cold and some of the sadness came off
on my skin. I felt like I had seen someone naked by accident.
I mumbled some magic words
and buried it back in the garden.

I found a magic ring digging in the garden, made of diamonds
and gold and rubies and plastic. I didn't know what its powers
were. Then my ears grew longer and longer like pink ribbons

my fingernails grew in spirals
and I remembered
it was mine all along. Remembering was its first power.

I found a pair of eyes in the garden, dripping wet in the evening
rain. They were wedged between the lavender fingers
and green hearts of the lilac, shaking like a vibrato
in the downpour, optic nerves clinging
to the smallest branches.
Even with the dangling capillaries
blood clots and blind spots, I
knew they could be saved if I tried my best. I
lifted them, cooed to them, cuddled them and coddled them
between my breasts like a goddess
and they rolled around in my gorgeous mess,
tangled in the blanket of my hair, my heartbeat
strong and fair and able
to provide
shelter.

THE STAR AND THE CROP

In the glassy dark of the horse's eye I can see a woman drawing her hair back and fixing it at the nape of her neck. She bows her head, kneels by a small pool, and immerses a copper vessel in the water. She stands and lifts the pitcher skyward. I can't hear her over the murmurations of the carnival, but her lips are moving, chanting in the night of the iris. I can see the words, points of light floating from her mouth like fireflies. They flutter across the threshold and tumble down each Arabian eyelash, slipping out into the world holding hands, knitting a blanket to soften the sting of the whip.

THERE IS A MOTHER WAITING
FOR YOU, A KANGAROO

You can't feel it yet, but there is a mother
waiting for you, a kangaroo

with glossy black eyes and ears that curl forward at the sound of
your voice. She lives in a cave beyond the jungle of your betrayal,
your repentance, your forgiveness. Beyond the desert of words and
needles, the thorns and flowers of your loneliness, the cities that
still burn with the riots of your love and the ocean you refuse to
remember.

She calls you in the mother tongue
you thought you had forgotten

and watches you stumble forward through the shadows. She nods
and you sit at her feet. She smells like her body. She holds the truth
in her pouch, amber light flowing through the white fur of her belly.
She passes it between padded paws and black claws, palm to palm,
a smile playing on her whiskers.

Late as you are, wrong as you are, she has never
given up on you, has kept something

warm for you. You are a baby, you are a brat, crying, begging her
for a bloody nose. She gives it to you with a cheerful kick and then

another for asking, eyes full of the you that you don't understand.
She pulls you close and dulls the pain with the sound of her voice,
clicking, chattering, licking you clean, her warm pink tongue
flickering soft and steady over your face, your eyes, your hair, your
eyes.

You confess, undress. She helps you out of your lies
and your jeans, listens
as if it matters because it matters to you
and you crawl ever closer
to the light, almost ready
to climb
in.

POCKET HOLLOW

Do you know what June meant
when she said *surrender,*
when she shrank smaller and smaller
until the periwinkle bluebells
of her sundress fluttered down
like a broken parachute,
when the string of glass cornflowers
clattered to the kitchen floor?

Do you know why she laughed,
scrambling skin and knees
down the wicker wedge and sandal straps,
why she walked straight to the body
of the man in the black silk coat
climbed up his arm
tiptoed across his chest
and slipped into his
inside pocket?

I don't doubt that it's soft
on her tiny white cheek,
on her naked fingers,
on her wrist, curling down.

SHE COMES IN ON A PEAHEN

Landing heavy on the railing
a satin saddle fastened
around the belly of the bird.

She's the size of a newborn
but she's a full-grown woman
in her way, steel blue corset offering
shiver night sighs above and below, fire
escape rattling rust in the snow
Don't go, she says.

The bridle hangs loose, glinting silver
in the streetlight beak to back.
Her chin tilts warm and her tiny arms
circle the animal's neck,
peacock feathers in her dress
and Krishna-crested crown
Fly away, you say.

She laughs at your nerve and you
notice her belt, the knife and violet
velvet satchel her night eyes
close as she reaches in

and pulls out a fistful of light,
hissing pink from between her fingers.
You wish it not to be true.
For you, she says.

As usual, you back away
from the window, notice how the wind
moves the hair on your arms
and the fringe on your pretty little lamps,
your soft artificial light

Her lotus fingers open,
the light dies down and
you forget yourself, climb
outside to see and *smack!*

Shame in a blanket,
beggar in a sheet,
a tattoo you, blue lines
blinding down to stories
playing out in tiny movies
on the palms of her hands. Only shadows
understand tattoo cartoon you,
you last year last week
crying lying and
so selfish

The monarch caterpillar eats its skin
each time it molts
but you refuse to consume your past,
accuse her with your slippery eyes.
You slip in, slam the window
and run to your bed
Coward, she says.

Real goddesses grant wishes for free,
you cry, as if you didn't know

She is also you,
casting off from the rail,
fire eyes skyward.
Icicles fall to the street
tinklecrash as the wings open
jump into the wind and she
flies up past the rooftops
beyond every light but never
disappears.

THE WAY THE WORLD ENDS

Night snow swirled in streetlight clouds. At first I thought it was a barrel of whiskey strapped to the back of the gangly old man, stooping him over to half in the parking lot. As he shuffled closer, I realized it was an egg, yellowish, enormous, bound with dirty ropes around his dirty coat. There were scratches on it as long as my arm, and I wondered whether they came from the inside or the outside. I loaded the groceries into the car and pushed my cart at him through the slush.

"That's not how it works," he said. "I have to carry it myself."

SEVEN NOTES

The music beats them down and lifts them up, bliss and throb. You are absent, thrashing, spinning free. You swing along, a plaything flying through whirlpools, floating blindly with the rest— then, seven notes, seven notes of now run down the canals of your ears like desperate prophets, scrawling graffiti on the inside of your ribs, your spleen, your belly. "No," write the seven; "Yes," write the seven. "You," write the seven, "are not here," write the seven.

All at once, you remember the music, your music, the dream that breathed you from nothingness to being. You feel a lightness in your chest, a sigh lifting you above the dizzying mob; then you are back, the booming rhythm clashing with peals of heart and thunder, your arms dropping dead at your sides.

Across the floor, she keeps swaying, but her eyes are open, watching you. She heard the same seven notes. She saw you stop, and she knows why.

Beyond the oil slick abalone lights playing dark windows, stretching floor to ceiling in the ballroom, you can see the real light of the moon, struggling through the clouds. You have to get out.

You heave through the crowd, heavy with the gravity of voices echoing down the hollows of your gut, your openings, your knees. You stumble, bangles catching on velvets and lace. The dancers screech and spin over the edge of chaos, dresses and hair, arms and ornaments whipping.

You are suffocating. Thunder crashes louder than the beat. Lightning flashes beyond the glass, calling you to push.

You are outside. The door closes, dampening the volume of the dance. You lean against the wall of the night sky. Even in the rain, the moon is beginning to show her face. Cool raindrops patter down your forehead, your cheeks, your painted lips, dripping off your chin. You run your hands over your face and head, snagging strings of hair-twisted jewels that fall to the ground.

You breathe. You feel the full weight and distance of just how long you have ignored your song, and the vast gap aches.

The music blares again and she storms through the door, hands on hips.

"Your precious *music*, your stupid *song*! It's nothing! You love it so much, more than anything, any*one* in the world!" She is crying. The rain comes harder, louder, turning the edges of her hair into perfect little ringlets around her face. Her glittering eyes grow even bigger, yellow eye paint and violet diamonds shining, lashes grasping, irises brimming like laps of mercury. Even her weeping is exquisite, and she knows it.

Seeing those eyes fill with rain is almost too much, but the music has opened a door in you, a door you can't close, not again.

You turn away and slam your palms against the wall. Cold pain rings warm. "You're lying. If it's nothing, why is it forbidden? Why can't I sing it? What kind of love is that?" You picture yourself

42

crumbling, your back sliding down the wet wall, your face puddling into your knees. You refuse, shaking, summoning everything you have to keep looking her in the eye.

"All I've ever done is protect you. What have I ever denied you?" Her hands are on your shoulders, her warmth melting your resolve. Her lavender velvet sleeves coil around your arms, twisting into snakes on your wrists.

"Only this," you say, pulling free before you disappear. "Only the only thing that means anything."

"Then I am nothing?" Thunder. It's torrents, coming in sheets now.

"You are nothing! I am nothing!" You're grateful to the pounding rain that lets you sob, lets you admit it out loud, lets you yell your loudest.

"You are someone," you read on her quivering lips. "You are Beautiful. You are my Beloved."

You deflect the blade of her love, twisting it sharp. "Your love is not Love," you say, closing your eyes. "Tell me what you know about the music." Love has its own rules, and she knows them too. She looks away.

"All I know is that it will kill me."

You wish she were lying. The seven notes are growing dimmer, huddled together in the corner of your left lung. They bang their heads gently against your walls.

"No more talk of the music," she narrows. "Choose between me and the music!" You see her as your jailer again. The hatred that has always rippled through your love for her swirls to the surface.

She just stands there, shaking in the thunderstorm. She hugs her arms around herself, her best velvet soaking wet. "Choose," she says again, but she knows you already have.

You reach out to touch her, but she tears away from you, eyes full of pain. "Watch me die, then."

The rain burns her down, sizzling away her magnificent hair first, the paint on her perfect cheekbones, the gems on her temples. You are surprised that her body, once so substantial, can evaporate so fast. You know the feel of it, how tight to hold her, where to kiss her, how far apart her eyes are. You almost want to save her, to catch her clothes as they collapse empty on the ground. At first, the seven have to prop open your lungs, pulling from ropes lassoed to your collarbone. Then you remember the music.

THE GOBLIN KING SLIPS AN EMPTY STRING

With a noose knot on the hole of you. Look at him, all owl feathers and magic tricks, costumes and dreams, a liar in the land of the living walking on the ceilings of time. Masquerade balls and erotica boots work on your weaknesses, blackmail your truth with your vanity, measuring you for fitting. He sings to the things you think you are, illusions orbiting colors you can't see with eyes so wide. The crystal ball rolls up the stairs, bait for your monstrous desire. He wants his woman to fear him. You must be starving: beauty or not, that's no peach.

THE WATERFALL

Behind it, you will find the treasure, they said. They provided the approximate dollar value, the exchange rate, and the map to the mountain. They gave you moral support and told you, even before you could understand, that you would grow up to be a fine climber, like your father. They taught you everything you would need to know to complete the journey: how to buy good rope; how to wear tight boots with spikes in the soles; how to carry a heavy pack, with all its ties and sharp little hooks. We believe in you, they said. Your father didn't make it, but you will. We will be so proud of you, and that will settle the debt of our kindness.

Resist all your urges: the urge to scream, the urge to run, the urge to kick holes in walls. The urge to tell her. But especially the urge that will come on the final switchback of the trail: the urge to fall.

Because when you can feel the water in the air, and the gravity is deafening, you will begin to think that it is soft. You know how sharp the rocks at the bottom are, you lost your own to them; but the altitude will get to you, and you will begin to think of letting go. You are tired of being a separate person, and it will feel like courage to drop away into the mist.

When you see the waterfall, the gold will glint shards of light to you through the icy curtain. You will know how close you are and you should, you should, you most certainly should. Only three small wet steps, three slimy little steps. You will hate yourself for listening to them, for growing old accepting their help and their food and their map. You will hate that they were right, that it worked and now you are here.

You don't remember your dreams in the morning, but they were there. You want the things you are not supposed to want. Close as you are, wet as you are with spray and sound, the dark matter in you will try to close the wound, expanding the universe in your belly, exploding and birthing stars with forces you don't understand. It will tell you to disappear.

Resist.

THE WEST WING

We'd barely set down our suitcases when Vic said he wanted to leave. "Let's wait for a Howard Johnson. This place is a dump. Look, cockroaches!"

And there they were, pausing to give us the once-over as they strolled across the Pepto-pink bedspread. "Yes," I said, "but they're dressed to the nines."

They were stunning, her in an ivory ball gown with puffed sleeves and a train made from the iridescent wings of flies, and him in his coat and tails and tiny top hat.

"Let's stay," I said. "Maybe we can learn something."

"Don't be stupid," Vic said. "Roaches are roaches."

THE LADY SCARECROW

The love poem is on the other side of the hate poem. It hangs from the wrist of the bald lady scarecrow, a white-skinned mannequin with rose madder lips and rhinestones in her eyes. She wears my old nightgown, the stained one. She lives in the wild of the yard.

It tries to escape, spinning on the line, on the rusted hook that went in easy through titles that used to mean something. Catch and release is not as clean as it sounds: there are barbs. The skin is different, between bruise blue and gray and green, but the eyes and the bleeding are the same.

The gusts throw and it lands on stars. Roll again: suffer. Blow: the purple pen you bought for me, the red felt tip I stole. Purple flips and blurs red, both bleeding through. We hung it as a joke, like when you laugh about the time you broke your ankle. Still I will feel better when it rains again and I hope it melts into pulp and falls in the weeds at her feet. Even now I am pretending I will forget.

Her fingers turn out, her wrist on her hip. She used to wear wigs and bracelets in showrooms. Her collarbone peels now with the weather. Still, I think she prefers the open, but it's hard to say: the hate poem is on the other side of the love poem.

SOFT FRACTURE

Like buffalo in the cornflower dawn steam nostril hoof hoof rising
the truth is already awake and if you could take off your shoes and
other favorite prisons you would feel the day tremble through
forget-me-not tallgrass prairie bluestem yarrow grief light humble
tender as lovegrass dew lifting lungs

to try again

ONCE UPON A TIME I DIED

Once upon a time I died. I crucified myself on a ladder built from the bones of birds, hollow, not yet cleaned by cannibals or the sun, yet flightworthy by nature. My vertebrae dissolved without the soft bits to hold them together, my rich cartilage collection of the fastest way to get to the airport and how much salt goes in curry and how to cut the baby's nails suddenly useless.

I trickled down, fell like beads when I cut my own string. Some days I can laugh at the little pearls, curling up like roly-polies. Some days I can't. Won't, I mean, but I don't have to be fair anymore.

My favorite thin cotton pillowcase and my favorite mug and the face I saw in a cloud in my Dostoyevsky days—what are they worth? I didn't want to laugh, some days. It's not funny when an ocean evaporates. Make a list, and another list, and another. I know it's a lie, but I want to touch them on the shelves.

I remember only the days of building, winding my hair around each rung, chanting *cancer, cancer, enlightenment, fault! Itsy bitsy alakazam! Ashes, ashes, we all fall up.* Don't we?

I took someone's word for it somewhere along the line, or I wouldn't have made this scaffolding in the first place, getting more precarious the higher I go. I had a blueprint, I know. It was on the fridge, sharing letter magnets with the boy's kindergarten drawing of all of us together and the grocery list and the photo booth pictures where we look so silly and free, before we knew. It must have blown off some night when I forgot the kitchen window open or whirled around after stepping on the cat's tail. But I had a plan. It was all very clear at one point, the instructions coming in snippets of radio songs, dreams and omens and the language of color behind closed eyes, the language of sunlight through lace curtains on the warm wood floor: *Spring comes, and the grass grows by itself.*

But will it come if I am full of rocks? They emerge from my palms, igneous, metamorphic and sedimentary: obsidian, slate, granite, marble, each with their own sharp edges, their own important veins. Graceless, they tumble, following the fragments of my skeleton down the dry riverbeds where I was born to build. I can wait a thousand years to reach the ocean if I know I am going, even piece by piece.

I would rather not, of course. Waiting and building and falling apart are not my way at all. To tell you the truth, it's not finished. I ran out of hair, I ran out of feathers, I ran out of funny and beautiful and brilliant and everything else I have used to bind you to me. What else do I have? How many days can I wait for the boiling point?

I give up, I give up: I tear free and jump. Fuck it, fuck it: I run. I run so hard I land in California, Mumbai, Mozambique. I take like a fire to the world, licking the crops of every continent black, wiping the slate clean with one snap of my neck like a dragon the size of a star.

And after the slash and burn, the land could breathe. In the early morning, before the new growth, I remembered the dream I had of freedom from my favorite jeans and my best work, and I was home in time to make breakfast from the ashes.

In my spare time, I am building a ladder with the bones of birds, hollow, not yet cleaned by cannibals or the sun, yet flightworthy by nature.

MARS KISSES CLING HARD

Mars kisses cling hard
in our bubble of alone. We are spiders
on a cellar door. We are too light
for gravity; we find a way in.

I could not change the television murder factories the lies the agony
lives bought and sold in rooms of rich men and the world kept on
spinning as I sang and changed diapers, sang and built a puppet
theater, sang and yelled and burned the rice and waves and wars
fluttered over the earth like dirty comforters and clean sheets,
fighting outside what fought inside, the clear breath of day that
burrows down tornado holes into shrapnel yet I have seen it come
out the other side as muddy paw prints, streaking evening gift
sunsets, together naps and forgiveness and whatever I have been

my boy has the guts to wrap his arms
around this red red planet
and play.

THE FISHERMAN'S GAZE

Light comes the moment
the flame touches the feather,
yellowed with the oil of her hands.

The fisherman's gaze
crosses his pale porcelain catch
landing on her fingernail
as she closes her eyes to iron.

She lays hands on the soil,
pulling the blight up
through her palms.

She eats lead.
She stirs the pot.

When the cloud hums up her arms,
rising like a fever to her cheeks
and rolls out the almond door
of her mouth

Canoes burn clean
and the way is made clear
for the bonsai.

THE WIDOW'S CAT

I found a black widow shaking in the bedroom, sitting in the morning sun on the windowsill. She was mumbling the rosary in a small, desperate whine, like a faraway train trying to stop. Through a white lace veil draped over her head and the top of her abdomen, I could see the silhouette of the little beads slipping methodically through her jointed forelegs. She became still and silent and turned to me, her eyes, two rows of four, clouded and quivering. A tiny tear dripped off the end of her fang.

"Don't worry," I told her, "there is no Cat."

THE MASTER

I was dancing with Rachael, who died twelve years ago in June. It was a soft, soft room with velvet orange-red carpet, and we were going crazy, laughing and whooping faster and faster, eyes-locked mirrors winging to the rockabilly, perfect loud. We kicked off our flips to feel the shag. There was no window in there, no time. I thought I could leave and come back anytime.

It was afternoon when I closed the red door on the music. I was standing on an upstairs landing of the kind of place that's crowded with houseplants, the kind of place where you feel safe to play. From the long windows, sunshine painted hardwood stairs, five feet wide and broad, stretching down to the first floor without a railing. I bounded down: *bam bam bam bam bam!*

When I got to the bottom, I remembered my flips. I turned around, but on the middle stair sat a monk in orange robes with a shaved head. He was speaking to a dozen people in pastels, crowding around cross-legged or crouched, hanging on the stairs with their cloth bags and water bottles, straining to hear his voice.

At the bottom was the Master, in white, amused and aloof, enjoying himself. He was sitting in a white armchair with his ankle on his knee, and his beard was dark gray, like the early days. We sat together like friends. "I need to get my shoes," I said.

He smiled. "You will have to wait," he said. "You will have to wait and listen."

THE EDGE OF THE WOODS

No one has even asked if I'm ready.

You must be ready, or you wouldn't be here. I can carry that for you.

Thank you. I'm not sure if I am ready. Which way?

We just follow this path in, and then left at the fork, past the lightning tree.

Is this the lightning tree? Can we stop for a minute?

Almost everyone stops here at the fork. The shine is oil from all those hands. Go ahead, touch it.

It's warm, and so smooth. How is it warm in this chill, in this dim light? There are colors here—are they moving? It looks like a cottonwood, but it can't be. Is it dead or alive?

Hard to say. Are you an artist?

Yes.

That can make it harder. Or easier. What kind?

What kind of artist? All kinds. A real artist uses everything she can get her hands on, doesn't she?

I suppose so. Would you like to paint right now?

No.

How about writing? I bet you're a poet, too.

I am, but there's no point in putting it off. This isn't a pleasure cruise. Let's get on with it.

You're the one who said you weren't ready. There's a piano just down in the valley there if you'd like to play.

A piano out here in the woods?

Yes. Careful, those rocks are loose. Take my hand.

Oh! I wish I had a camera. Just look at it, nestled in the leaves like it grew there. It looks like an antique. Is that a real owl on the lid?

Yes, that's Sophie. She's come to see you off.

I love owls. Look at her, so calm, so close! Maybe I will play for a minute.

Easy. The bench is rickety.

You look like a barn owl, Sophie. Do you know this one?

That's a wonderful melody, like the ocean, like waves crashing on the shore. What is it?

Nothing. I mean, I'm making it up as I go along.

Sophie likes it. I've never seen her sit so still like that.

I think she knows me.

Yes.

I think I know her, too.

Yes. Why did you stop?

I'm ready.

GRANDMA'S EGG

There is a consciousness, an awareness in the smallest crumbs of quantum particles. Without names or eyes, they know when they are being watched. Cities of cells and symphonies of light ebb and flow with their own mysterious rhythms.

What is magic? What is the transmission of the lamp? Is it simply waiting for another microscope, some stronger math to make it visible to our naked eyes?

Oils from my grandmother's fingers left her body when she smoothed the stationery. Did she touch the oak desk? How much of the forest had it brought with it to her little house? What did she touch before she touched the paper—*Lemony Snicket*? The phone? The piano? *A Room of One's Own*?

No, she must have been at the kitchen table, by the window in the morning sunbeam, light falling in her hair, sliding from distant stars at great speed over her forehead and playing down her nose, absorbed into her, her grip casting a shadow on the paper. Did she set down the pen to lift the teacup with her right hand, or did she use her left? No one can understand how hard it is to live not knowing whether it was the right or the left, or whether she touched her lip, or whether she propped her chin in her hand, elbow on the table. There is no one I can trust for the answer.

She paused to look out the open window, of this much I am sure. She moved a strand of hair behind her ear. A bird alighted on the bush, and the genus and species in Latin, as well as the common name, flew unbidden to her mind: *Spizella Passerina. Chipping sparrow.* "Well, hello there!" she would have said, and the vibration of the music of her voice rattled the image on her retina, the sparrow hanging upside down inside her eyes like a bat. Then, she would have sipped her tea to return to the task at hand, not realizing that the combination of sight and sound had taken flight, seeping through blood and bone and tissue and hitching onto her fingers when she touched her temple. She had to decide what to write and what not to write, and she may have thought nothing more of it as she smoothed the stationery and the oils from her fingers and one cell from her temple left her body and became part of the letter. Then again, maybe she knew.

She held the paper in her left hand. She read it over again, pointing with her right, checking for spelling and punctuation. She folded it with both hands, sliding thumb and forefinger down the width of it, and put it in the envelope. By then, the blue-gray ink of her favorite pen knew her as she wrote my name. What did she give me? What was she humming as she licked the envelope?

The first day, the letter sat on the coffee table, and the next day it sat on the kitchen table. That is where it was when the juice spilled, and I screamed at the baby; that is where it was when the ink ran, and I tried to blot it dry with napkins. That is where it was when I tried to make it flat again, and it began to warp.

It was wavy at first, a rectangle of water frozen in time. The table was full of bills and toys and something that needed fixing, and it was moved to the side, and then the back corner, and then the table was full of groceries that needed putting away, and I stopped thinking about the letter.

The next morning, as I made breakfast, the baby crawled under the kitchen table. "Ba," he said, lifting up a gray-blue egg the size of his hand. "Mommy, ba!"

"It's not a ball," I said, amazed. I peeled it out of his fingers. "It's an egg."

I held it in both hands. Grandma had been diagnosed. Her swooping, luxurious handwriting swirled diagonally across the widest part of the oval, distorted but still legible. It was warm. It was alive. I should have been more careful, I thought. I should have kept the letter safe. It was my scatterbrained life, my unconsciousness, my fault.

I was not at home when it hatched. I had gone to see her one last time. When I returned, my beloved told me that the chipping sparrow was born complete, flying, not a helpless, featherless, bug-eyed rat looking for someone's regurgitation. She was sharp and fast, and she trilled with bliss. She flew not for duty, not for instinct, but for joy, to chatter in the baby's ear, to dance through the air, teasing me, tempting me with life, opening my eyes and keeping me company.

Does it matter that I smiled when the letter came, that I touched it with my palms, that I smelled the envelope after I tore the top? What combination of particles lingered on my fingers—stray cells from the rice? The bed? The baby? My beloved, or my own salt? And now, after so much skin has been shed, how much of that ink remains in my bloodstream?

I wanted to keep her forever, to break the rules of nature as she had. I wanted to find a cage big enough to hold her, but she was too strong, too free. The apartment was too small for her. She began to gaze out the window, and I finally had no choice but to open it. She looked back once over her shoulder, and flew away.

GOOD DREAM BAD DREAM

With the right eyes
you can glide over the lambent magnetosphere
amber rose sapphire black ice
truth and beauty and the heartless nothing
beyond the veil
see city lights so far below
and still find your way home.

CHAPTER TWENTY-SIX: THE MAP[1]

By the end of the first day after coming over the top of the range, I was scrambling down reddish boulders and walking on rocky soil instead of crystals. I stayed that night under a gathering of old long-needled pines that tempered the hard rain into soft plinks by the time they reached my little tent. I painted by candlelight, trying to capture what I had seen from the top—not only for the beauty of it, but to make a map. I rolled it up and kept it in an outside pocket of my pack.

One thing I had not seen, even from that height, was the Indigo Desert. I had no reference points left, no way to calculate where the birth city might be. There was nothing in all the colors and patterns and shapes I had seen there that was familiar, and my mind argued that the logical thing to do would be to go back over the crystal range and search for the city in another direction. Seeing that vast unknown, though, I had the belly feeling that it knew me, somehow, that it was on my side, that something would catch me if I fell blind into the new wilderness below.

The next morning was warm, and I awoke feeling at once calm and wild, thrilled at the prospect of having no idea what the day and this new land would bring. I chewed rosemary as I moved slowly down through the valleys, going up again when there was no other choice, and it was in this way that I found her.

---

[1] This piece is an excerpt from *Oma*, a novel-in-progress

She came into my vision without warning, just as the sun came to the crest of its climb and I came to the crest of mine at the top of a ridge. I immediately crouched behind some scrub oak, more from surprise than fear. My blood was racing, and I shivered even though I was sweating in the thin mountain air.

At least fifty rough stairsteps were cut into the steep, rocky slope on the other side, which led down to a round meadow of wildflowers. The ground was dashed with blasts of color—firewheels, moonflowers, black-eyed susans, scarlet trumpets, bluebottles. A Chinook warmed me suddenly and rolled down the ridge, and the blossoms below floated and bobbed on a sea of green.

The clearing was ringed with trees, white-trunked aspens with black lines and knots like eyes, the same in kind as those that had been with me for days. These were taller, though, and their leaves were still a grassy green, vital and alive, unlike their yellowing cousins on the mountain behind me. Their leaves whispered in the breeze.

She was in the center of a circle inside the circle, immersed in her work, squat-walking backward in patterns of small, fast steps and delicate, deliberate actions. She was short and fat, and her position made her look even shorter and fatter. From my vantage point, the top of her head of white dreadlocks, piled high and wide in a spiral bun, seemed suspended in the middle of the purple cotton-covered rounds of her body. She looked like a huge lavender daisy herself, a queen mother of flowers, her tiny children dancing near and far in the soft, warm wind.

I watched the thick, waddling woman work in fascination, untying my load. Something about her was otherworldly, almost frightening, but I couldn't put my finger on why. Hands appeared intermittently from beneath her big violet petals with a knowledge all their own, moving to different places on a makeshift tool belt while her gaze remained fixed on the ground in front of her. The belt around her midsection was fashioned with funnels that held perhaps twenty different cone-shaped bags of sand. Each one was a different color, ranging from white to periwinkle to iridescent indigo, and I recognized each shade and tint from the desert I had crossed so long ago.

She was making something. The inner circle of shorter grass she moved within was about ten paces across, and as I watched, an intricate pattern began to emerge, folding and blossoming, rising and falling with waves of color and design. She lifted each colored canvas cone with a strange combination of concentration and thoughtlessness, absolute presence and absolute absence, as if she weren't really there at all and the sand painting was painting itself. She held each cone at a different distance from the earth, sometimes letting the sand that fell through the tiny hole in the bottom pile into round pyramids and sometimes not. Then she pinched it quickly, folding it over and putting it back in its funnel. Sometimes, on a periwinkle pile, she drizzled a smaller white pile and then a midnight blue one; sometimes she trickled thin lines, shuffling backward, which curled into spirals. Other lines were straight.

Mesmerized, I watched her imagination come to life. As the circle of sand inside the circle of flowers inside the circle of trees became more and more complex, the lines and dots and piles of ultramarine and cerulean crossing swirls of peacock blue and turquoise, I began to think she must not be touching the ground at all. There was no place left to stand, much less squat and shuffle backward, without ruining the design, yet she kept on pouring sand and switching cones with the same fluid movements and the same speed, never tripping or scuffing her work.

The vision of her creation was intimate, familiar. It seemed to match something that was already behind my eyes, or lower in my body, something I had forgotten was there. The painting was not symmetrical, and yet it was; it was not logical, pure whimsy, pure play, yet it described order, and not a grain of sand seemed unnecessary or luxurious. It was like a song for the eyes, without words, expressing everything that I wished I could say, but could not. Something dripped on my breast, and I realized I was crying.

I touched my cheek and looked at the sky. The sun had passed me by and set behind the pines, winking from deep between with oranges and reds. I looked quickly back to the meadow, terrified for a moment that I had imagined the whole scene, but there she was, scuttling backward, shifting cones and drizzling sand even faster than before. Then, in the middle of the circle, she stopped. She stood up and took in her creation, hands on her hips like a sundial, her long shadow telling the time. She turned slowly in a circle, and then looked straight up at me. "Come," she said. Her voice was low but clear in the silence of the mountains. "Let's eat."

And with that she turned her back, scattering a path through the sand, walking straight through the painting as if it were nothing but a desert. I grabbed my pack and rose to follow, leaving the map behind.

NIGHTSHIRT

It was shocking to find the moon to be just as Billy had always seen her in books: the pointy chin, drooping lids and blue glitter eyelashes, the silver curlicue smile. Cold as it was, she smelled like steamed milk, and the look in her eyes was warm and vast, outside and inside at the same time. She was almost two-dimensional, but he knew she had room for him. He climbed on, nestled his knees into the hollow under her bottom lip, hooked a hand around the bridge of her nose, and fell asleep in the pillow of her cheek.

CIRCLE, HEART, CROCODILE, RIVER

In the dream she is naked, a brown silhouette on the not-yet sunrise floating down over the skyscrapers, the string to a blue paisley kite in one hand and a cigarette in the other. She draws deep and blows out rings: circle, circle, heart; circle, crocodile, river. They move and swim through the cold light, chasing each other until they disappear in the clouds.

You rise to your feet on the rain-clean cement of the sixth-story roof, climb up the clothesline and try to balance on the wires. You can make out her eyes as she comes closer, just low enough. You jump onto her legs, cling tight and drift with her: building, building, neighborhood; building, city, ocean. Her body is made of chocolate, and you can't stop yourself from licking her knees.

She laughs, and you lick harder, then try a nibble, then a bite. She is so sweet, so rich, so smooth that you don't see her take one last drag, sigh out a smoke feather, and lift the eye of the ember to the edge of the kite. Flames race around the hem and spines. She doesn't melt; she burns, and disappears, and you plummet into the sea like a comet, your mouth full of ash.

In real life, at the party, the same paisley decorated her sari, dripping with glass beads, cobalts and mercury, a waterfall that night from her widow's peak to behind her ear. The lock of hair that had escaped, curling past her silver eye to rest on her cheek, whispered a promise that it could all be undone: the hair, the gold, the sari, the tight midnight blouse. You could imagine those little hooks, and you wondered if they were in the front or the back. You should risk everything and talk to her like you know her, you thought. You should tell her that you want to see her with her hair down, that the time has come for her to open her every corner to you. She should forget herself and cover her mouth, or smile and touch your hand, or look around the room to see if anyone noticed the blood blush in her cheeks.

You are a coward, and you might not have done it. It was the night-blooming jasmine, you told yourself later. It was the wine, the opium, the heat, unusual for spring, even in Mumbai.

You called her with your mind and she came to you through the crowd, unblinking. You should have noticed how she seemed to move without walking. You should have noticed that the tea lights on the far side of the room flickered out when she spoke, back on the mantle where her hand had been before. That the peacocks stopped calling when she opened the garden door and took to their roosts in the banyan trees. You did notice, but the sari was sheer, and the drift of her hips and the shadow of her navel made you forget.

She gave you what you wanted behind the fountain, the parrot trees, the statue of Shiva, at once dancing the world into being and dancing it out of existence. Her eyes slipped closed, lips parted. Yes and yes and again yes, she said, until you could ask no more.

The craving for her other corners faded, then, and again you followed your desire, this time to run through the garden door and out the other side, tossing her empty promises.

You are free now, except for the dream. There is nothing to fear, you tell yourself one day in the marketplace, when a hunchbacked old woman catches your eye. First it's the sari, a paisley, cobalts and mercury; then it's the way she seems to move without walking. Then she is holding your hand.

"Can I help you?" you ask, just rude enough to disguise the shaking.

Her grip is tight, and her silver eyes invade you. "Yes."

I'M BUILDING A HOUSE ON THE
RAILROAD TRACKS

You're coming. Cheek to the rail I feel
your rumble.

I'm building a house on the railroad tracks
out of matchsticks box nails and one-way glass,
the dried Valentine's Love-Lies-Bleeding
with no past address.

I will cut this pillow
for the embroidery meadow.
I'll rip the sheet from my mother
for the arc of the rainbow,
tear the hummingbird skirt
from before we met.

I'll cut my silk bathrobe
with the Great Wave on the back,
the tiny fishermen in their tiny boat,
the wave so big the water has teeth and

my curtains will be so beautiful

I can keep them closed while I wait.

PUBLIC POEMS BUILT ON PUBLIC PROPERTY

Public poems built on public property are, as they say, asking for it. When you use such flimsy bread, eating away at holy Wonder until such thinly-sliced letters remain, every one meant to be swallowed, not spoken; when you hold them down with found rocks in a stream that is not a stream, just a concrete ditch void of the hand of God; when you slip out the window in the night like a Sufi thief or an idiot child, praying the wrong way, dancing naked and licking vowels in your own nonsense language

don't expect to get anything

except

arrested.

THE GOLDEN THREAD

1

It's too dark. I heard there are tigers in this jungle.

Yes.

Ordinary tigers?

No, they're faster, and their fangs have venom, like a snake.

What if we see one?

They will see you first. Just watch. Just be still.

How can we be still with tigers after us?

They're not after you.

What if they catch me?

*If you run, they will chase you, and they will catch you. They tear
the throat, and the poison goes in the blood. It paralyzes you, makes
you blind, makes you forget why you are here. And then you drop
the thread.*

2

I can't see. What's that smell? Some sweet jungle flowers. Are we
getting close?

No, it's poetry, a copycat fragrance. Stay back—

Those are my words on the vines! God, those electric blue letters!
Let's read—

Don't—

Why? "Once upon a time I died. I crucified myself on a ladder
made from the bones of birds, hollow, not yet cleaned by
cannibals or the sun, yet flightworthy by nature." I wrote that.

You can't see, but it's full of teeth—the vines, the leaves, even the petals. Especially the petals.

No, it's soft. My poem is a flower! What do the petals say?

Let go!

Oh my God! My head is bleeding. How did it bite me so fast?

Poetry is like that.

Maybe we should go back. My head hurts, and I can hardly see, and... tiger!

3

Just relax. It's not after you.

It's coming. I can't breathe. It's going to get me. Maybe it is me, maybe I am the tiger. I always knew it.

Be still. You can breathe. It's not you.

I can feel the blood on my fur, I can taste it. I have to get away!

There's nowhere to go. Running won't help, I told you. The only way is to be still and watch.

It's watching me, too. Is it stopping? I can hardly see.

Yes. Just wait.

I'm not a tiger! I was just...

It's ok. Do you have the thread?

No. I don't even know where I lost it.

See the glow from the poem? Look there.

I can see where I dropped it. I think I have it.

Hold it tighter. No, in your left hand. Do you really want to go in?

Yes.

Then you can. Come back to the path.

4

But what about the tiger? It's still watching me.

Get out of your headache. Move down into your feet, and we won't need to worry about the tiger. What does the path feel like?

Fine, dry dirt, smaller grains than sand. Soft. My feet sink in with every step. I can't remember the last time I was barefoot outside.

Don't try to. Is the path warm or cold?

Cool, like morning, just before the sun comes up.

Any rocks?

No, not on the path. It's getting lighter.

Yes.

Look! What is that? Is it snowing?

We're getting closer.

The trees are gone—where are these flowers falling from? It's like slow motion. God, what are they? White, white, no, pink. And the smell is like...nothing I've ever smelled before. There are no words for it.

This is the real thing.

I think I lost the thread again.

You don't need the thread anymore.

Where are you?

You don't need me anymore.

WOKE UP THIS MORNING

Older than words
older than light
every bit born
in the bellies of stars
I am the light behind my eyes
that doesn't show in pictures,
only in the mirror.

I saw for myself
that when everything is off
I am the dirt from the Garden of Eden.
If I dig I have seen it,
I have been there which means
I am there
just forgetting it all the time
leaving it all on
turning it up louder
pushing up daisies and video games
I am there except that I'm not

If the flower is contained within the seed
and the seed within the flower,
what's the point in blossoming?

There must be a side road
some backwoods path through the long grass
'cause if it's all the same to you
I could pass on the suffering in between

Woke up this morning
so far from home
wildflowers in my eyes
birds in my bones

I am just a verb, a happening
like lightning or a laugh or a storm
but even a storm is a someone
capable of harboring life
and some storms catch their own rainbows
and lock them up for further study

It's too slippery
you can't catch me
you can't step in the same river twice,
can't step in the same me.
I am swollen with rain
and I dried up in the drought
forever babbling and long since silent
I am lost in ten thousand eddies
and I have already reached the ocean.

I had the visions I know
I think I had a vision
I think I used to know
I have magic x-ray glasses I swear
I just forgot them somewhere

Woke up this morning
in the river alone
guess I sank in the night
drunk and blind as a stone

How long will I be able to pull it off?
like a cloud's shadow on a mountain
I am mostly empty space
pretending to be somebody.
Even the mountain is a cloud.

Maybe I don't appreciate the mystery
I don't groove on gravity,
just enough to keep us
from flying off
but that's exactly where I'd rather be
in zero G
free of the pull of the soil
the toil the tread the
aching bread
the bodies that tend to fall

towards the center of the earth

Woke up this morning
my head in the clouds
same blues as last night
same blues as the crowd

Everything I do makes a mark
I am changing the universe forever making
snow angels on cosmic carbon paper
a novel written on water
but written all the same

They say you can't hear sound in space
but all our lovesongs float away intact
sail on radio waves, crossing paths
with the billion-year-old past light
we still think is real

If matter is not created or destroyed
only energy changing form
what's the difference?
I'm not eating my peas,
just moving them around.
I was the garden
now I am the gardener
next time I want to be the boots

I can't draw a line around my body
I don't know where I stop
when I drink the tea,
can't touch the moment
when it becomes me
when the cat purrs on my lap
when you purr on my lap
I disappear

Woke up this morning
coming down from a dream
I drowned in your eyes
trying to swim upstream

The war in love
between somebodyness and bliss
is the fight inside the tide
I want to dissolve in the ocean
like salt like a star
winking out at dawn
I want to evaporate I swear
melt into the night of your arms
without the fear of getting lost

But when that tide goes out
it's my war against yours,

a Dead Sea scroll stretched
between us, wound around
at both ends

Woke up this morning
naked, broken and blue
throat full of heartache
head full of you

I cannot grasp eternity
I am not clear on my place in the galaxy
but I think it moves faster than light and
gets nowhere
like me

Maybe those glasses weren't magic,
just some cheap crap from a cereal box.
maybe the vision was just a dream,
a memory of a movie twisted
by my desire to be somebody who can see
space is not completely empty but
I can't see a damn thing in this darkness

Woke up this morning
remembering this song
cried myself to sleep
and now the fear is gone

Lightning cut the tree while I was sleeping,
lightning cut open the belly of the sky.
Stars fell down with rain and I
was shaken to the roots,
wind knocked out of me knocked free

from words and light,
eyes washed real with pain
and only with the fall to earth
was I able to see the way

to awaken.

WE ARE APRICOT TREES

We are apricot trees, male and female

In the blossoming when bees carried
me to you on their legs, pink-white
petals and yellow pollen
tickling in the wind

In the giddy firsts of nesting,
robins' eggs speckled with flight
and the music of the future

In the in-between, all our sap
given to the fruit, so many lost
to hail and squirrels,
arsenic pits moving away
through raccoons down the alley

In the sickness when bark beetles
peeled us open, laid eggs in our wounds
and ate our insides out

Still you and me in the thinning
fall, faced with who we are not,

wrong in layers
of wet skeletons but

Even in this frozen sleep
our roots touch underground
with every possibility
of awakening.

ONLY FLYING

It was not until it hit the blade of the catastrophe rock, littered with femurs and water skulls, that the river split open and found the leverage to jump out of its bed. It left the comfortable moss, the minnows' gossip, and the sound of its own body rubbing past stones, on or around. It surrendered, leapt without choosing, a reflection in air of the path it had known before—the meadow, the factory, the wooden swing. The cottonwoods, black and white. It had become the ocean it had always wanted to meet, silent now, still flowing down the same path. Only flying.

WITH GRATITUDE

I would like to thank my beloved Man, Gaurav Bhagat, for dancing with me and flying with me and catching me when I jumped off busses and helping me become myself. You are my par'mach'kai.

My children for playing with me and loving me back and helping me grow up.

My parents, Jeanne and Danny Higham, Jerry and Lucinda Pebley, and Nirmala Balani, for believing in me, nourishing me in so many ways, and helping me find the time and space to write this book.

My little sister, Robin Higham, for her love, support, last-minute feedback as a writer and as a friend, and her everlasting gifts of listening and coffee.

My big sisters, Arati Sharma and Prerna Khanna, for their love and friendship, and all my family in India for welcoming me with open arms.

My writers' group, The Nearby Universe, especially Amie Sharp and Carina Bissett, for the motivation, friendship, and fabulous late-night feedback.

My teacher and friend, Kelli Allen, for her endless encouragement and feedback and for showing me the path to publishing and to the Weird.

All my wise, joyful teachers, especially Carla Dolan, who works and lives from the heart, never asking for anything in return.

My students, past, present, and future, for listening to me, challenging me, laughing at my jokes, and giving me a reason to get worked up about writing again and again.

The amazing team at Unsolicited Press, especially my editor, Alexandra, for her insight and excellent suggestions; Katie, for the breathtaking cover; and Summer, my managing editor, for her understanding, and for going above and beyond.

Finally, though the internet has told me not to do it, I want to thank you, dear reader, for catching the other end of the soup can telephone I'm tossing out the window. It doesn't work without you.

ACKNOWLEDGEMENTS

"The Lady Scarecrow" and "My Nothing Burned Down to the Center of the Earth" were previously published in *Lamplit Underground Magazine*. "Once Upon a Time I Died" was previously published in *Lotus-Eater Magazine*. "The Same Woman (Scarlight)" was previously published in *Monkeybicycle*. "Downwelling" and "She Comes in on a Peahen" were previously published in *Harbinger Asylum*. "Woke up This Morning" was previously published in *The Syzygy Poetry Journal* and *Quail Bell Magazine*. "Pocket Hollow" was previously published in *Rat's Ass Review*. "I Get Found, 1974" and "I Found a Pair of Hands Digging in the Garden" were previously published in *Empty Mirror Magazine*. "Nightshirt," "The West Wing," "Public Poems Built on Public Property," "Wavestar Bang," "The Way the World Ends," "The Left Eye Is Enough," "The Goblin King Slips an Empty String," "The Golden Thread Part I," "The Golden Thread Part 2," and "Only Flying" were previously published in *A Story in 100 Words*. "Grandma's Egg," "Sailcloth," "There is a Mother Waiting for You, a Kangaroo," "The Edge of the Woods," and "The Star and the Crop" were previously published in *Peacock Journal*. "Jump (Magic Pants)" was previously published in *MoonPark Review*. "Good Dream Bad Dream" was previously published in Beth Boldman's article about micropoetry in *Pandora's Box Gazette*. "There is a Mother Waiting for You, a Kangaroo" was previously published in *Peacock Journal — Anthology: Beauty First [Volume II, Number I]*.

About Brook Bhagat

Brook Bhagat's poetry, fiction, non-fiction, and humor have appeared in *Monkeybicycle*, *Empty Mirror Magazine*, *Harbinger Asylum*, *Little India*, *Rat's Ass Review*, *Anthem: A Tribute to Leonard Cohen*, and other journals and anthologies, and she is the 2020 winner of *A Story in 100 Words'* nature writing contest. She and her husband Gaurav created *Blue Planet Journal*, which she edits and writes for. She holds an MFA from Lindenwood University, is an assistant professor of English at a community college, and is writing a novel. See more at brook-bhagat.com or reach her on Twitter at @BrookBhagat.

About the Press

Unsolicited Press was founded in 2012 and is based in Portland, Oregon. The small press publishes fiction, poetry, and creative nonfiction written by award-winning and emerging authors. Some of its authors include John W. Bateman, Anne Leigh Parrish, Adrian Ernesto Cepeda, and Raki Kopernik.

Learn more at www.unsolicitedpress.com

CPSIA information can be obtained
at www.ICGtesting.com
Printed in the USA
LVHW111731261021
701609LV00004B/202